To:

_____

With Love:

_____

Published by Christian Art Publishers
PO Box 1599, Vereeniging, 1930, RSA

© 2020
First edition 2020

Designed by Christian Art Publishers

Images used under license from Shutterstock.com

Scripture quotations are taken from the *Holy Bible*, New Living
Translation, copyright © 1996, 2004, 2015 by Tyndale House
Foundation. Used by permission of Tyndale House Publishers, Inc.,
Carol Stream, Illinois 60188. All rights reserved.

Printed in China

ISBN 978-1-4321-3124-1

22 23 24 25 26 27 28 29 30 31 – 18 17 16 15 14 13 12 11 10 9

Prayers

FOR MY
BABY GIRL

Carolyn Larsen

CHRISTIAN ART
PUBLISHERS

God's Precious Handiwork

O GOD,

Thank You for shaping every detail of this precious child within me. You already know everything about this little one.

O Father, surround this child with Your love and protection. This little one, Father, is Yours, not mine but I thank You for allowing me to have the privilege of being her parent.

In Jesus' name,

AMEN.

You made all the delicate,
inner parts of my body and knit me
together in my mother's womb.

PSALM 139:13

KNOWING GOD EARLY

Father,

I pray that this precious little one will come to know You early so she can spend much of her life learning to know You and serve You.

Guide me as I teach her about You. Father, help me be a good model of Your love and care.

Father, don't let me get in the way of her knowing You. In Jesus' name,

Amen.

You have been taught the Holy Scriptures from childhood, and they have given you the wisdom to receive the salvation that comes by trusting in Christ Jesus.

2 TIMOTHY 3:15

Courage to Try New Things

DEAR GOD,

Father, begin preparing this child for the future by planting curiosity in her heart. Provide opportunities to explore new things as she grows.

I pray that she will have courage to step in to opportunities to use the talents and abilities You have given and that her efforts will bring more awareness to this world of Your love and care.

In Jesus' name,

AMEN.

"Don't be afraid, for I am with you.
Don't be discouraged, for I am your God.
I will strengthen you and help you.
I will hold you up with My victorious right hand."

ISAIAH 41:10

CARING ABOUT OTHERS

Dear Father,

Help me teach my child to remember to be kind and considerate of others. Even as she moves through her younger years when children can be so self-focused, show me how to point her toward generosity and kindness.

Help me model humility as I teach her what it means to be a kind and respectful person who values others' feelings.
In Jesus' name,

Amen.

Don't be selfish; don't try to impress others.
Be humble, thinking of others
as better than yourselves.

PHILIPPIANS 2:3

True, Lasting Peace

DEAR FATHER,

Fill my child with peace. I pray that her heart's peace will come from trusting that You hold each day of her life in Your loving hands. Peace comes only from knowing You.

I pray that this precious child comes to understand that and hold onto You early in her life so that her heart will be at peace.

In Jesus' name,

AMEN.

You will keep in perfect peace
all who trust in You,
all whose thoughts
are fixed on You!

ISAIAH 26:3

MY HIDING PLACE

O Father,

Protect this girl from all
who would try to hurt her, not
only physically but also emotionally.
Protect her from believing hurtful
words. Help me keep communication
open with her so that I can encourage
her when she's hurt or lonely.

Most of all, keep her close to
You so she always knows she's
loved and protected.
In Jesus' name,

Amen.

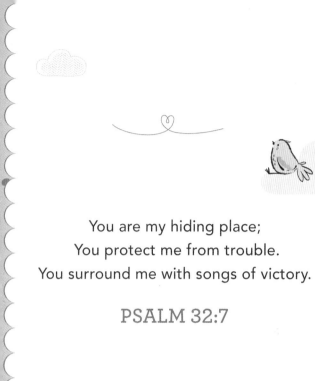

You are my hiding place;
You protect me from trouble.
You surround me with songs of victory.

PSALM 32:7

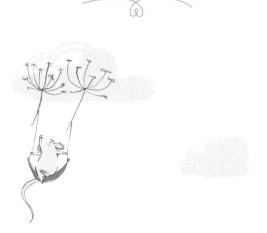

God, the Waymaker!

DEAR GOD,

You are the Maker of pathways, the Guide to purpose-filled life. Your Word says You already have a plan for my child's life. Guide her path.

Direct her choices in friends and activities to those who will bring her closer to You and keep her from any temptations to turn away from You.

In Jesus' name,

AMEN.

"I know the plans I have for you," says the LORD. "They are plans for good and not for disaster, to give you a future and a hope."

JEREMIAH 29:11

GOD'S CREATIVE POWER

O Lord,

You intricately shaped and formed this new life inside of me. In just a matter of weeks my child's heart was beating and she was already a living being.

Everything her body needs to grow into a complex, active, intelligent adult is already in her tiny body. Every blood vessel. Every muscle. Every cell.
O God, You are amazing, and creative.
In Jesus' name,

Amen.

Thank You for making
me so wonderfully complex!
Your workmanship is marvelous -
how well I know it.

PSALM 139:14

Needing God's Help

DEAR FATHER,

I'm holding this tiny human but I do not feel ready for the responsibility of being her parent.

What if I don't know enough? What if I don't have patience? What if I make mistakes? I want to parent her well; to teach her to know You, and to love others. Show me how, Lord. Teach me so I can teach her.

In Jesus' name,

AMEN.

Commit everything you
do to the LORD.
Trust Him, and
He will help you.

PSALM 37:5

A KIND HEART

Father,

I pray this child will develop a kind heart that looks at others with compassion.

I pray that she will stand in the gap between bullies and victims and seek to lift up the bullied with encouragement.

Father, help her be kind when others aren't; give of her time and emotions; consider others more than she considers herself.
In Jesus' name,

Amen.

Since God chose you to be the holy people
He loves, you must clothe yourselves
with tenderhearted mercy, kindness,
humility, gentleness, and patience.

COLOSSIANS 3:12

God's Promised Help

DEAR LORD,

This child was Yours before she came to my life. I'm honored (and a little nervous) to have the responsibility of raising her. I can't do any of it without You.

Thank You for trusting me with her. Thank You for the gift of her. Help me, guide me and keep me leaning on You, trusting You and following You.

In Jesus' name,

AMEN.

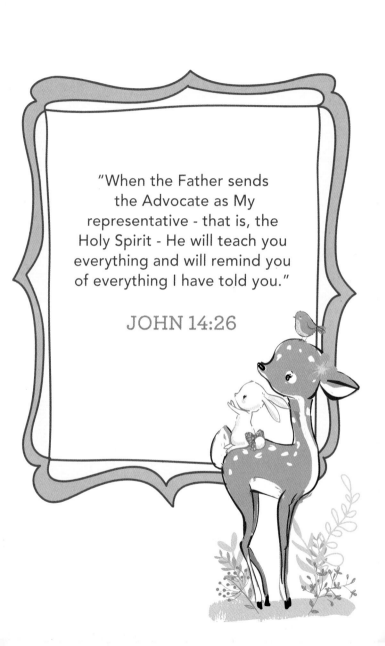

"When the Father sends the Advocate as My representative - that is, the Holy Spirit - He will teach you everything and will remind you of everything I have told you."

JOHN 14:26

MODELING JESUS' LOVE

Dear Father,

From now on every word I speak, every attitude I project will be observed by my child. I want her to know the joy of following You.

Help me remember that her eyes are watching and her ears are hearing. Keep that foremost in my mind so that whatever she sees in me will reflect You to her.

In Jesus' name,

Amen.

Live a life filled with love, following
the example of Christ. He loved us
and offered Himself as a sacrifice for us,
a pleasing aroma to God.

EPHESIANS 5:2

Encouraging Words

O GOD,

I know I have control issues so I ask You to warn me when I'm trying to control her life. Keep me from stifling the person You want her to be.

Help me encourage her interests even if I don't understand them. Help me enjoy the adventure of her becoming the girl and woman You have made her to be!

In Jesus' name,

AMEN.

Let us think of ways to motivate
one another to acts of love and good works.

HEBREWS 10:24

DEEP, DEEP LOVE

Dear Father,

Even before my baby was born I loved her with all my being. I can't imagine life without her. I'd willingly give my life for her.

I pray that my daughter will always know that she is deeply, unconditionally loved, by You and by me. May she believe and trust both of those deep loves with no doubts. In Jesus' name,

Amen.

We love each other because
He loved us first.

1 JOHN 4:19

Never Give Up

DEAR GOD,

I know my child will experience failures, or at least things she considers failure. Those are painful times.

Father, help her discover early in her life that failures are opportunities to learn and grow, not for giving up.

Help her know that failures don't mean the end. Keep her moving forward and learning.

In Jesus' name,

AMEN.

He said, "My grace is all you need.
My power works best in weakness."

2 CORINTHIANS 12:9

COURAGE TO BE
AN INDIVIDUAL

Dear Lord,

Help my daughter avoid the temptation to compare herself to her peers. I pray that she will see her own uniqueness and embrace it.

I pray that she will not settle for being one of the look-alike, act-alike pack. Give her the courage to be herself! In Jesus' name,

Amen.

I am certain that God, who began
the good work within you, will continue
His work until it is finally finished on
the day when Christ Jesus returns.

PHILIPPIANS 1:6

Send a Good Friend

DEAR FATHER,

I pray my daughter will cultivate friendships with Christians who serve and honor You. Friends who will challenge her to stay true to You and encourage her to serve You.

I pray for friends who will lift her up when she stumbles and will stand beside her in loyalty and defend her when necessary.

In Jesus' name,

AMEN.

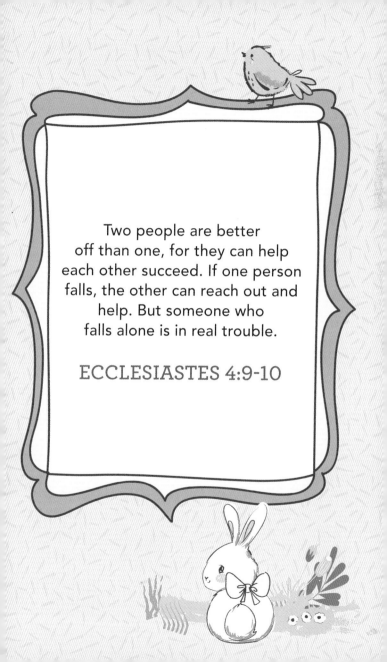

Two people are better
off than one, for they can help
each other succeed. If one person
falls, the other can reach out and
help. But someone who
falls alone is in real trouble.

ECCLESIASTES 4:9-10

PRAYER FOR FORGIVENESS

O Father,

I long to be a perfect parent but I know I won't be. Father, help my child know that I'm trying. Plant forgiveness in her heart when I'm impatient, critical or selfish.

I pray that my shortcomings will never make her question my love. Give me the courage to admit my failures so that she can learn from my vulnerability.
In Jesus' name,

Amen.

Be kind to each other, tenderhearted, forgiving one another, just as God through Christ has forgiven you.

EPHESIANS 4:32

Sacrificial Love

DEAR FATHER,

Thank You for this child and the privilege of being her mommy. I don't take it lightly. Having her in my life gives me new understanding of the magnitude of Your love in sending Your only Son to earth for me. What a sacrificial act of love.

Thank You for this child, another evidence of Your great love.

In Jesus' name,

AMEN.

Love never gives up, never loses faith,
is always hopeful, and endures
through every circumstance.

1 CORINTHIANS 13:7

THE PRIVILEGE OF PRAYER

Father,

Teach my child the power of prayer.
Help her know the blessing of talking
with You about anything and trusting
that You hear her prayers
and care about them.

I pray she will know the privilege of
sharing in others' lives by praying
for them too. I pray her relationship
with You will grow deeper through
communication in prayer.
In Jesus' name,

Amen.

Don't worry about anything; instead,
pray about everything. Tell God what you need,
and thank Him for all He has done.

PHILIPPIANS 4:6

Stay Close to God

DEAR FATHER,

Someday my girl may be bombarded by people claiming they know truth — but it won't be Your truth. Guard her heart, Father. May the truths of Your Word take a firm hold in her heart.

Protect her and keep her heart close to You so that she will know real truth.

In Jesus' name,

AMEN.

Come close to God,
and God will come close to you.

JAMES 4:8

BLESSING OTHERS

Dear Father,

Help this child learn that life is not all about her. Keep her from being tempted to think that even the talents and gifts You've given her are for her own enjoyment and success.

Show her how to use those things to serve others and draw them to You and to enrich their lives.
Give her a helpful heart.
In Jesus' name,

Amen.

God has given each of you
a gift from His great variety
of spiritual gifts. Use them well
to serve one another.

1 PETER 4:10

Lifting Others Up

DEAR FATHER,

Help me teach my child the dangers of comparing herself to others. Help her see the problem of pushing others down in order to elevate herself.

Help me model an attitude of humility and submission to You. Help her become a woman who finds her worth in You and because of that can celebrate the successes and joys of others.

In Jesus' name,

AMEN.

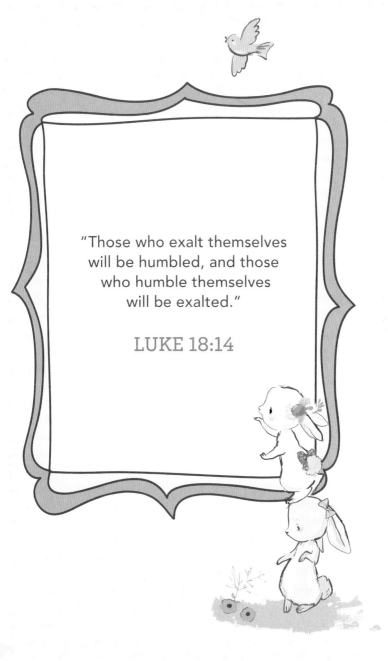

"Those who exalt themselves will be humbled, and those who humble themselves will be exalted."

LUKE 18:14

SERVING AND BLESSING OTHERS!

O Lord,

Bless this precious new life
with a tender heart filled with
compassion for others. Bless her
with a spirit that looks for ways to
serve and help others.
May humility guide her, not pride.

Lord, may she become a woman
of God who seeks to serve You and
those around her. Give her wisdom
to know how to do those things.
In Jesus' name,

Amen.

Blessed are those who trust in the LORD and have made the LORD their hope and confidence.

JEREMIAH 17:7

Hands That Serve

DEAR FATHER,

I hold these tiny hands in mine and wonder what this child's future holds. I pray these little hands will be used to serve You. Guide these hands to ways to make life for all on this earth a little better; a little gentler.

Lord, whatever this child's future holds, may these tiny hands be used for big service to You!

In Jesus' name,

AMEN.

Whatever you do or say, do it as a
representative of the Lord Jesus,
giving thanks through Him
to God the Father.

COLOSSIANS 3:17

PROTECT
HER HEART

Dear Father,

Guard this little one's heart.
Protect her from Satan's tricks.
Help her grow into a girl and
then a woman who loves You and
is submitted to You in all her
thoughts and actions.

I pray that Your angels will be an
army around her, keeping Satan from
her so that as she matures she will
still be choosing You.
In Jesus' name,

Amen.

Stay alert! Watch out for your
great enemy, the devil. He prowls
around like a roaring lion, looking
for someone to devour.

1 PETER 5:8

Making Memories

DEAR LORD,

Help me make memories with my child. Remind me how quickly her young years will pass. Help me push aside things that keep me from making time for her. Help me be creative in how we spend that time.

Help me make time to play and even be silly sometimes so that as she grows she will have wonderful memories of childhood.

In Jesus' name,

AMEN.

Let all who take refuge in You rejoice;
let them sing joyful praises forever.
Spread Your protection over them,
that all who love Your name
may be filled with joy.

PSALM 5:11

DESTINY BY GOD'S PLAN

Father,

I believe You have a plan for my daughter. You made her perfect in Your eyes – just as You planned for her to be. Thank You that even before she entered this world, You had a plan for her life.

I pray, Lord, that she will seek to follow that plan and be open to wherever You lead her.
In Jesus' name,

Amen.

"I knew you before I formed you
in your mother's womb.
Before you were born I set you apart
and appointed you as My prophet
to the nations."

JEREMIAH 1:5

Hunger for the Word

FATHER,

I pray that my daughter will have a hunger for Your Word. I pray that early in her life she will understand the power of Your Word and the benefits to her life of knowing Scripture.

I pray that she will be diligent about hiding Scripture in her heart so that it's always at the ready to help her in her life.

In Jesus' name,

AMEN.

I have hidden Your
word in my heart,
that I might not sin
against You.

PSALM 119:11

BREAKING
THE PATTERN

Father,

Our world has become so publicly negative about anyone who holds different viewpoints. Please remind me of this when I'm tempted to jump on the negativity bandwagon. Remind me that little ears are listening.

Help me model kindness so that my child may one day break that pattern by her words and actions; loving others as she loves herself.
In Jesus' name,

Amen.

"Love the LORD your God with all your heart, all your soul, and all your mind. This is the first and greatest commandment. A second is equally important: 'Love your neighbor as yourself.'"

MATTHEW 22:37-39

Lifelong Trust

DEAR LORD,

Help my daughter keep her childlike trust in You as she grows up. I pray that she sees Your protection and care in her life and learns that she can trust You to care for her and guide her throughout all her life.

Keep her focus on You so she's not tempted to place trust in anything or anyone else.

In Jesus' name,

AMEN.

Trust in the Lᴏʀᴅ with all your heart; do not depend on your own understanding. Seek His will in all you do, and He will show you which path to take.

PROVERBS 3:5-6

BE STILL

Father,

In this busy, high stress life,
help me model that it's good
to practice stillness.

Give me the vulnerability to be still, be
quiet, be prayerful so that she can see
the value in those actions and make
stillness a practice in her life, too.

Then she will have opportunities
to hear Your voice and know
Your presence in her life.
In Jesus' name,

Amen.

"Be still, and know that I am God!"

PSALM 46:10

Filled with God's Strength

DEAR FATHER,

Fill my child with Your strength. Give her the persistence and endurance to withstand temptations, to stand strong against those who would try to pull her away from her own beliefs and morals, or would discount the value of living for You.

I pray that Your strength in her heart will give her all she needs to stay true to You.

In Jesus' name,

AMEN.

Those who trust in the LORD
will find new strength.
They will soar high on wings like eagles.
They will run and not grow weary.
They will walk and not faint.

ISAIAH 40:31

KEEPING COMMUNICATION OPEN

Father,

Help me keep communication open with this child. Help me listen deeper than her actual words and hear the emotions behind them.

Help me make time to not only hear her but to engage in conversation. If I do that when she's young, the pattern may be established to keep the communication going as she grows. In Jesus' name,

Amen.

Ears to hear
and eyes to see -
both are gifts from
the Lord.

PROVERBS 20:12

Choosing Joy

DEAR FATHER,

I pray my daughter learns to be grateful for the gift of life each day. Help her resist being pulled down into negativity through focusing on problems that keep her from seeing daily blessings.

I pray that she sees me start each day with expectation and joy and true gratitude for life and that she will learn to do that, too.

In Jesus' name,

AMEN.

A glad heart makes
a happy face;
a broken heart
crushes the spirit.

PROVERBS 15:13

FOCUSED ON JESUS

Dear Father,

I pray my daughter will always keep her eyes on Jesus and that she will learn early in her life to turn to Jesus for guidance, wisdom, comfort and strength.

Help her resist the temptation to push Jesus aside and trust in other people or situations. I pray, Father, that she will stay true to You in her trust and devotion. In Jesus' name,

Amen.

Oh, the joys of those who do not
follow the advice of the wicked,
or stand around with sinners,
or join in with mockers.

PSALM 1:1

A Good Strong Will

O FATHER,

I pray that this child's strong will becomes a strength that helps her be true to herself. May this strength keep her from following a crowd mentality.

I pray that the desire to have friends or to fit in with a crowd will not overpower her. Protect her, Father, through her own strong will.

In Jesus' name,

AMEN

May the Lord lead your hearts into
a full understanding and expression
of the love of God and the patient
endurance that comes from Christ.

2 THESSALONIANS 3:5

WORRY IS A WASTE OF TIME

Father,

Help my daughter learn that worry uses up energy and is often about things that she can't control anyway. Help her learn that worry shows a lack of trust in You.

Help me be her teacher on this by modeling trust in You rather than worry. It's not always easy, but with Your help I can be her example.
In Jesus' name,

Amen.

"Can all your worries add a
single moment to your life?"

MATTHEW 6:27

Whatever God Plans

FATHER,

I pray that this child You are forming inside me will be healthy and strong. I pray for physical and mental strength that will lead this child to a wonderful future.

But, Father, if You have something else planned for this child, then prepare my heart to accept it and to trust You with whatever happens because I trust Your love.

In Jesus' name,

AMEN.

You saw me before I was born.
Every day of my life was
recorded in Your book.
Every moment was laid out
before a single day
had passed.

PSALM 139:16

NEVER ALONE

Dear Father,

I pray that my child will know
the joy of never feeling alone. I pray
for close family relationships, even
when we disagree about things.
I pray for good friends who will
support her and challenge her.

Most of all I pray that she realizes
You are always, always with her.
Thank You for Your constant
presence in our lives.
In Jesus' name,

Amen.

"I am with you always,
even to the end of the age."

MATTHEW 28:20

Living Worship

FATHER,

I commit to taking my daughter to church, reading the Bible to her and praying with her. However I know that worship is a heart response to who You are and what You do for us.

I pray that my daughter will learn to prepare her heart for worship and expect to meet You in those experiences.

In Jesus' name,

AMEN.

I plead with you to give your bodies to God because of all He has done for you. Let them be a living and holy sacrifice – the kind He will find acceptable. This is truly the way to worship Him.

ROMANS 12:1

A LIFE DEDICATED TO KNOWING YOU

Dear Father,

Of all the things I could pray for this child, the most important is that she will come to personally know You. I pray that she will give her heart to You at a young age.

I pray that her faith and trust in You will grow stronger and deeper with each year so that her life will be dedicated to serving You.
In Jesus' name,

Amen.

"This is how God loved the world:
He gave His one and only Son, so
that everyone who believes in Him
will not perish but have eternal life."

JOHN 3:16

Parenting with God's Wisdom

DEAR LORD,

Give me Your wisdom in guiding and teaching my daughter. Give me patience and a sense of humor. Help me appreciate her joy in learning, even when she makes mistakes.

Give me the wisdom to spend time with her because I know these years will go by quickly. Help me be the kind of mom she needs!

In Jesus' name,

AMEN.

If you need wisdom, ask our
generous God, and He will
give it to you. He will not
rebuke you for asking.

JAMES 1:5

CONFIDENT HUMILITY

Dear Father,

I pray that my daughter will find that sweet balance between confidence in how You made her and the gifts and talents You have given her versus self-pride that pushes others down. It's a fine line. Guide her in that.

Teach her how to have confidence mingled with humility and the strength to lift others up.
In Jesus' name,

Amen.

Pride leads to disgrace,
but with humility
comes wisdom.

PROVERBS 11:2

Respect-Filled Fear

DEAR FATHER,

Help my daughter develop a deep and healthy respect for You. I pray that she will realize that while You do love her, You also have standards, commands and morals which she must obey. Not to obey is sin.

I pray that her understanding of Your Word will grow so that her obedience will grow and that respect-filled fear will keep her obedient.

In Jesus' name,

AMEN.

Fear of the Lᴏʀᴅ is
the foundation of
true wisdom.
All who obey His
commandments will
grow in wisdom.
Praise Him forever!

PSALM 111:10

A GIFT OF LOVE

Dear Lord,

I pray my child will realize how much You love her. Your love is evident in the precious gift of Jesus dying for her sins.

Help her see that she didn't have to do anything to become worthy of that gift. Jesus loved her and died for her before she even knew His name! Help her see His sacrifice of love.
In Jesus' name,

Amen.

God showed His great love for us by sending Christ to die for us while we were still sinners.

ROMANS 5:8